INTRODI

Edward Hasted was born on Decem[ ] [ ]
Edward Hasted of Hawley, in Sutto[ ] [ ]
father was a wealthy barrister whose fa[ ]
his father, Joseph Hasted (1662-173[ ] ...as Chief Painter to the
Royal Navy at Chatham. It was through Joseph's skill in the financial
markets that he amassed a large estate that yielded an income of £1,000 a
year. The Hasted's came from an ancient Kentish family, branches of
which are recorded in Canterbury's registers as far back as 1540.

Between 1740 and 1744 Edward was educated at the King's School in
Rochester, after which he spent the following four years at Eton,
completing his education with by two years at a private academy in Esher,
Surrey. On leaving school in 1750 he briefly followed his father's
profession as a lawyer and spent a short period as a member of Lincolns
Inn in London.

Edward's father died unexpectedly at the age of 38 and the family
subsequently moved to Rome House, near Chatham. In 1752 Edward
returned to the old family home at Sutton-at-Hone where, in 1755, he
married Anne Dorman, the daughter of a near neighbour. It was at this
time that he began gathering the material from which he was to write "The
History and Topographical Survey of the County of Kent", the first
edition of which was published by Simmons & Kirkby of Canterbury, in
four large folio volumes, between 1788 and 1799.

The publication was well received and before the fourth volume was
issued Hasted begun work on correcting, revising, and extending the
entries in the earlier volumes in order to produce a popular edition of his
history in a more convenient octavo size. The smaller volume size meant
that the books could be sold at a far cheaper cost than the large tomes of
the first edition and hence they appealed to a much wider, general
readership. It is from volume III of this second edition that this reprint of
the entry for the parish of Brasted is taken.

The first three volumes of the second edition were published in 1797 by
the Canterbury printer, W Bristow. Over the following four years another
nine volumes were issued, with the twelfth and final volume being issued
in 1801.

Such is the size of the work that Hasted spent the greater part of his adult life involved in gathering material and preparing the text for his history. His research began when he was still a young man in his twenties, and by the time the last volume of the second edition was published in 1801, he was an old man approaching 70. In between he had amassed a wealth of topographical material on the county from sources throughout Kent and London which filled more than 100 bound volumes.

No subsequent history of the County of Kent compares with the sheer size and breadth of content of Hasted's History. The twelve volumes of the second edition contain almost three million words, spread over 7,000 pages, containing an account of every parish in the county. This includes details of the prominent citizens of the area as well as a descent of the various manors and a history of the local church and clergy.

Hasted's achievement is all the greater when one considers the distressing personal circumstances surrounding his life between 1785 and 1807. During this period he left his wife of 30 years for the affections of Mary Jane Town. He was pursued by his creditors and subsequently imprisoned for debt. Following his release in 1802 he lived in poverty in a succession of cheap lodging houses until in 1807, his old fiend and patron, the Earl of Radnor, presented him with the Mastership of Lady Hungerford's Hospital at Corsham in Wiltshire.

Edward died at the Master's lodge at Corsham on 14th January 1812 aged 79. His son, the Rev. Edward Hasted, was present at his death and buried his father in the local parish graveyard. In 1929 a monument was erected at Corsham in Hasted's memory by Dr. F. W. Cock of Appledore with the support of the Kent Archaeological Society.

Hasted was a loyal son of Kent and considered his home county to stand "foremost in the rank of all others, so deservedly proud of its pre-eminence in every respect." His History is a fitting testimonial of his love for his county and the fact that no work of similar size and stature has been published since emphasises the magnitude of his achievement.

JOHN W BROWN

HASTED'S HISTORY OF BRASTED

compiled by
John W. Brown

LOCAL HISTORY REPRINTS

316 Green Lane, Streatham, London SW16 3AS

Originally published in 1797 by
W. Bristow of Canterbury, Kent
as part of Volume III of
The History and Topographical Survey of the County of Kent
by
Edward Hasted

This edition published in 1996 by
Local History Reprints
316 Green Lane
Streatham
London SW16 3AS

ISBN 1 85699 141 5

PARISH AND VILLE OF BRASTED.

ADJOINING to Sundridge weftward, lies the parifh of Brasted, called in the *Textus Roffenfis* Bradestede, and in *Domefday*, Briestede. It feems to take its name from the long narrow form of it; *brade*, in Saxon, fignifying length, and *ftede*, a place. Within this parifh is a diftrict, called, *The Ville of Brafted*, which is a *jurifdiction feparate* from any hundred, having a *conftable* of its own, the remaining part of the parifh being the moft northern part of it, called Brafted Up-land, is in the hundred of Wefterham and Eaton-bridge. The church ftands within the ville.

The VILLAGE of Brafted is fituated on the high road to Wefterham, which leads through the parifh weft-ward, midway between the two ranges of the chalk and the fand hills, to the former of which this parifh extends, about a mile in length. About a quarter of a mile fouthward of the village, the river Darent flows through the parifh eaftward, a little fouthward of which is the church, and near the foot of the chalk hill, Bra-fted-court lodge, within the hundred of Wefterham and Eatonbridge.

Near the eaft end of the village is Brafted place, fouthward from which is a large parcel of wafte, rough, and woody ground, called Brafted Chart common, extending for two miles to the fand hill, below which it extends for fome length into the Weald, where it has the name of *Brafted Weald*, in like manner as the other parifhes mentioned before; where, at the fou-thern boundary of it, is the eftate, called Delaware. The whole parifh, notwithftanding its great length, at no part of it exceeds a mile in width; the foil of it,

above

above the hill, excepting near the river, is but very indifferent, being near the northern hills chalky, and near the southern hills an unfertile sand; below the latter it is a stiff clay.

A fair is kept at Brasted on Holy Thursday or Ascension day, for horses, cattle, &c.

The MANOR of Brasted seems to have been formerly accounted an appendage to the manor of Tunbridge. It was part of the possessions of the see of Canterbury, before the Norman conquest; accordingly it is thus entered, in the record of Domesday, under the general title of the lands held of the archbishop by knights service:

Haimo, the sheriff, holds Briestede of the archbishop. It was taxed at one suling and an half. The arable land is ten carucates, in demesne there are 2 carucates and 24 villeins, with 16 borderers, having 12 carucates. There is a church and 15 servants, and two mills of 24 shillings. There is wood for the pannage of 20 hogs, and as much herbage as is worth nine shillings and sixpence. In the whole it was worth, in the time of king Edward the Confessor, 10 pounds, and as much when he received it, and now 17 pounds. Alnod, the abbot, held this manor of the archbishop of Canterbury.

Soon after the reign of the Conqueror it came into the eminent family of Clare, afterwards earls of Gloucester and Hertford, who held it of the archbishop of Canterbury in grand sergeantry; and there having been great disputes between the archbishops and these earls, concerning the customs and services claimed by the former, on account of these premises, as well as others, which the earls held of them in Tunbridge, Hadlow, and other places in this county, the whole was finally settled in 1264, anno 42 king Henry III. by a composition then entered into between archbishop Boniface and Richard de Clare, earl of Gloucester, in which it was agreed, that the earl should hold the manor of Bradested, by the service of being chief butler to the
archbishop

archbifhop and his fucceffors, at their great feaft of inthronization, and that he fhould do fuit for it at their court of Otford; and the archbifhop agreed, that the earl fhould receive of him and his fucceffors certain fees and allowances, as therein mentioned, whenever he, or his heirs, fhould perform this office, at fuch time as above mentioned.[c]

Richard earl of Gloucefter and Hertford died poffeffed of this manor, at his houfe at Efchemerfield, in this county, in the 46th year of king Henry III. whofe grandfon, Gilbert, died poffeffed of it in the 7th of Edward II. being flain at the battle of Bannockf-burne, near Strivelin;[d] and on the partition of the inheritance of his three fifters and coheirs, this manor, among other eftates in Kent, was allotted to Margaret, the fecond fifter, then wife of Hugh de Audley, jun. who not only fucceeded to thefe lands of her inheritance, but was likewife, in the 11th year of king Edward III. created in parliament earl of Gloucefter. He died poffeffed of the manor of Bradfted, in the 21ft year of that reign,[e] leaving an only daughter and heir, Margaret, then the wife of Ralph Stafford, who in her right became poffeffed of it.

He was fo greatly efteemed by king Edward III. that, among other marks of his regard, he chofe him one of the knights of the order of the Garter, at the firft inftitution of it; and foon afterwards, in his 24th year, advanced him to the title of earl of Stafford. He died poffeffed of this manor in the 46th year of this reign, and from him it defcended to his great grandfon, Humphry Stafford, who was created duke of Buck-ingham, anno 23 king Henry VI. and was afterwards flain in the battle of Northampton, fighting valiantly there on the king's part. From him it at length de-

[c] Regift. Chrift church, Cant. No. 177. See a further account of this compofition, under Tunbridge.

[d] Dugd. Bar. vol. i. p. 213, 751, et feq.

[e] Rot Efch. ejus an. Philipott, p. 65.

fcended

fcended to his great grandfon, Edward, duke of Buck-ingham, who, in the 13th year of king Henry VIII. being accufed of confpiring the king's death, was brought to his trial, and being found guilty, was be-headed on Tower-hill that year.

In the parliament, begun in the 14th year, though there paffed an act for his attainder, yet there was likewife an act for the reftitution in blood of Henry his eldeft fon, but not to his honours or lands,[f] fo that this manor, among his other eftates, became forfeited to the crown, at which time there appears to have been a park here, though as I find no mention of one after this, it is likely it was difparked foon afterwards.

This manor feems to have remained in the hands of the crown till that king, in his 31ft year, granted it to Sir Henry Ifley, and his heirs, by the name of the ma-nor, ville, and park of Brafted, to hold *in capite* by the fervice of the twentieth part of a knights fee, and the yearly rent of 5l. 2s. 3d. per annum, in exchange for the manors of Bradborne and Tymberden;[g] which ex-change was confirmed by the king's letters patent, un-der his great feal the year after.

By the act of the 2d and 3d year of Edward VI. the the lands of Sir Henry Ifley were difgavelled, but be-ing concerned in the rebellion, raifed by Sir Thomas Wyatt, in the 1ft year of queen Mary, he was attainted and executed at Sevenoke, and his eftates were confif-cated to the crown; after which the queen, by her let-ters patent, anno 1ft and 2d Philip and Mary, for the confideration therein mentioned, to be paid by William Ifley, eldeft fon of Sir Henry, granted and reftored unto him and his heirs, the manor of Brafted, and the rents of affize there, and all other lands, tenements, &c.

[f] Dugd. Bar. vol. i. p. 171. See a further account of the Staf-fords, under Tunbridge.

[g] Aug. Off. Box E. 18. and Rot. Efch. ejus an. pt. 4. The following account of this manfion is taken moftly from the late lord Dacre's papers.

which

which had come into her hands, by reason of the
attainder, in as ample a manner as Sir Henry held
them, paying to the queen yearly, at her manor of
Otford, 102s. 3d. for this manor;[h] which Wm. Isley
remained possessed of till the 18th year of the reign
of queen Elizabeth, when becoming greatly indebted
to the crown, in 3644l. and upwards, and others, an
act of parliament passed for selling so much of his lands
as would pay his debts, and by it the lord treasurer
and others were appointed commissioners for that pur-
pose, who next year conveyed the manor of Brasted,
and all lands and tenements belonging to it, to Sampson
and Samuel Lennard, against whom, notwithstanding
the above act of parliament, the attorney-general, in
the 21st year of that reign, brought an information in
the court of exchequer for seizing this manor, with the
lands belonging to it, in Brasted, into the queen's hands,
under pretence of their having purchased them without licence first had from the crown, they being held
at that time of the queen *in capite*; to which the Len-
nards pleaded the statute of the 18th queen Elizabeth,
before mentioned, which they alledged was sufficient in
law for the lord treasurer and others to sell the same,
without any other or further licence obtained of her,
and they had judgment against the crown on this plea.

In the 22d year of that reign, Samuel Lennard re-
leased all his right in this manor and premises, to
Sampson Lennard, who married Margaret, daughter
of Thomas, and sister and heir of Gregory Fynes, lord
Dacre of the South;[i] who, on her brother's death,
Sept. 25, anno 36 queen Elizabeth, without issue, became entitled to the barony of Dacre, which was ad-
judged to her in the 2d year of king James I. in as full
and ample a manner as any of her ancestors had enjoyed
the same; and her descendants, lords Dacre: this ma-

[h] See more of the Isleys, under Sundridge.
[i] See Chevening, for a full account of these families.

nor

nor continued in like manner as has been already more fully related under Chevening, down to Thomas Lennard, created by king Charles II. earl of Suffex, againſt whom the ſame claim was made by the daughters and heirs of his youngeſt brother, Henry, deceaſed, to this manor, as being of the nature of Gavelkind, but the earl of Suffex proved, that the manor and lands in Braſted were part of the poſſeſſions of Sir Henry Iſley, at the time of the diſgavelling act of the 2d and 3d of king Edward VI. and conſequently entirely free from the cuſtom of gavelkind from that time, in a trial held at the Queen-bench bar, in Michaelmas term, anno 1709, on full evidence, this eſtate to have been diſgavelled by the above act, and had thereupon a ful verdict in his favour.

Thomas earl of Suffex died poſſeſſed of this manor and the eſtate belonging to it, in 1615, leaving two daughters, Barbara and Anne, his coheirs, the former of whom married Charles Skelton, lieutenant general in the French ſervice, and the latter married Richard Barrett Lennard, eſq. of Belhouſe. They, in 1717, joined in the ſale of Braſted manor, with the reſt of their eſtates in this pariſh, to major general James Stanhope, who that year, being then miniſter of ſtate, was created viſcount and baron Stanhope, and next year, earl Stanhope. He died poſſeſſed of this manor, in 1721, and his grandſon, the Right Hon. Charles earl Stanhope is the preſent poſſeſſor of it.[k]

This manor is now charged with a yearly fee farm of 5l. 2s. 3d. to the crown.

BRASTED-PLACE is an eſtate here, which was once accounted a manor, and was heretofore called *Crowplace*, from the reſidence of that family at it, as it was before that called *Stocket's*, for the like reaſon.

Walter de Stocket, ſometimes written in records and old deeds Stoks, held this eſtate of the earl of

[k] Coll. Peer. laſt edit. vòl. v. p. 32, et ſeq. See more of this family under Chevening.

Gloucheſter

Gloucester as the fourth part of a knight's fee, in the reign of king Edward I. whose family bore for their arms, *Per pale gules and azure, a lion rampant argent, pellettée.*[1]

Simon Stocket possessed this estate in the next reign of king Edward II. and built a chancel in the church of Brasted, as appears by a deed of that time.

His daughter Lora carried this estate in marriage to Richard Boare, who bore for his arms, *Gules, a boar passant argent*, and was succeeded here by his son John, as he again was by Nicholas Boare, his son, who leaving an only daughter and heir, Joane, she carried this house and estate, called Stocket's, together with the chancel above mentioned, and certain land, called Boare's, to Thomas Crow the younger, son of Thomas Crow, of an antient family of Suffolk, who had before purchased lands in Brasted, in the reign of Edward IV.

From this family, who bore for their arms, *Gules, a chevron or, between three cocks argent,*[m] which coat was afterwards allowed to Giles Crow, of Brasted, by Robert Cooke, clarencieux, anno 1586, it acquired the name of Crow-place, and continued in the descendants of it till the latter end of the reign of king James I. when Mr. William Crow alienated it to Robert Heath, esq. afterwards Sir Robert Heath, then of Mitcham, in Surry, and successively chief justice of the common-pleas and King's-bench, who was, though born in the adjoining parish of Eatonbridge, descended out of Surry from John Heath, who was of Limpsfield, in that county. Sir Robert bore for his arms, *Argent, a cross engrailed, between twelve billets gules,* being his paternal coat. In one of the south windows of the Inner Temple hall, his arms, as chief justice of the common-pleas, depicted anno 1631, are a shield of four coats; 1st, *Heath*; 2d, *on a bend, between two cotizes inden-*

---

[1] Philipott, p. 65, 66; Book of Knights Fees, in the Excheq.
[m] Peacham's Comp. Gent. p. 239.

ted,

ted, three mullets; 3d as the 2d; 4th as the 1st; *over
all an efcutcheon of pretence, ermine, a fefs between three
foxes heads erafed.*"

He was a great fufferer for his loyalty to Charles I.
for which, being obliged to fly in foreign parts, he died
at Calais in 1649, and his body was brought over and
buried in this church, where there is a ftately monument erected for him and his wife. Margaret, daughter and heir of John Miller, gent. by Mary, daughter
of Henry Crow, gent. by whom he had feveral fons
and daughters who furvived him. After his death
this eftate continued fequeftred by the powers then in
being till the reftoration of king Charles II. when Edward Heath, efq. his eldeft fon, took poffeffion of it,
in whofe family it continued till Sir John Heath, leaving by Margaret, daughter of Sir John Mennes, knight
of the Bath, an only daughter and heir, Margaret,
fhe carried it in marriage to George Verney lord
Willoughby, D. D. afterwards dean of Windfor, who
was defcended of the family of Verney, feated, in the
reign of king Henry VI. at Compton Murdock, in
Warwickfhire, where Richard de Verney, the poffeffor
of it, then built a noble manor houfe, the prefent feat
of the family;° who bear for their arms, *Three croffes
recercele or, a chief vaire ermine and ermines.*

His defcendant, Sir Richard Verney, flourifhed in
the reign of queen Elizabeth and king James I. He
married Margaret, daughter of Sir Fulk Grevile, by
Elizabeth his wife, daughter and coheir of Edward
Willoughby, efq. eldeft fon of Robert lord Willoughby,
of Broke, and at length heir to her brother, Fulk Grevile lord Broke of Beauchamp's-court, in Warwickfhire, and dying in 1630, was buried with his wife, at
Compton above mentioned, which from this family
acquired the name of Compton Verney. His younger

n Vifitation Co. Kent, 1619. Guillim, p. 293.
° Coll. Peer. vol. vi. p. 549, et feq. Dugd. Warw. p. 435.

son

fon, Richard, of Belfton, in Rutlandfhire, fucceeding to it at length on the death of his nephew, William, fon of his eldeft brother, Sir Grevile, without iffue.

After which he refided at Compton, and was knighted in 1685. In the firft parliament of king William and queen Mary he was chofen in parliament for Warwickfhire, and being a defcendant, through the female heir of Grevile, from Robert lord Willoughby of Broke, as has been already mentioned. he made his claim to that title in parliament, in 1695, anno 8 William III. which being allowed, he had fummons to parliament accordingly, and took his feat in the houfe of lords, according as the antient barons of Broke were placed there, who were originally fummoned Aug. 12, 1492, anno 7 king Henry VII. and dying in 1711, was buried at Compton Verney.

He was fucceeded by his fecond, but eldeft furving fon, George, D. D. afterwards dean of Windfor, and lord Willoughby de Broke, who married Margaret, daughter and heir of Sir John Heath, and in her right, as has been already mentioned, became poffeffed of this feat in Brafted; which his great grandfon, John Peyto Verney, now lord Willoughby de Broke (who, in 1761, married lady Louifa North, daughter of Francis earl of Guildford, by whom he had feveral children) alienated fome years ago to the Right Hon. lord Frederick Campbell, as he did not long afterwards to John Turton, efq. M. D. who is the prefent owner of it.

DELAWARE is a feat of great antiquity, fituated in the fouthernmoft part of this parifh. It was the refidence of gentlemen of this name as early as the reign of king Henry II.[p] of whom Robert Delaware was the laft, who, about the latter end of king Edward III.'s reign, died without male iffue, fo that Dionyfia, his daughter, became his heir, who carried this feat and

[p] Philipott, p. 137, by old evidences then in the hands of Mr. Seyliard.

eftate

estate in marriage to William Paulin, of Paulin's, in this parish; in whose descendants it continued till the reign of king Henry VI. when William Paulin, having an only daughter and heir, Elenora, married to John Seyliard of Seyliard, in Hever, she entitled him to the possession of both these seats. His descendant, of the same name, resided at Delaware, and was created a baronet in 1661, who bore for his arms, *Azure, a chief ermine*, which was the antient paternal coat of this family;[q] and among the Harleian manuscripts in the British museum, is the pedigree of Seyliard, of De la Ware, set forth, anno 1578, and continued to 1630. From him this seat descended to Sir Thomas Seyliard, bart. who about the year 1700, alienated it to Henry Streatfield, of Chidingstone, esq.[r] whose great grandson, Henry Streatfield, esq. of Highstreet-house, in Chidingstone, is at this time intitled to this estate.

CHARITIES.

WILLIAM CROW, esq. gave by will, in 1618, to the parish an alms-house, which was exchanged for the present workhouse, now vested in the parish.

ELIZABETH SMITH, alias CRANE, gave by will, in 1638, a house, vested in the parish, of the annual produce of 5l. 13s. 4d.

WILLIAM NEWMAN, gent. gave by will, in 1736, land, for cloathing the poor, vested in the ministers and churchwardens, of the annual produce of 12l. 8s.

BRASTED is within the ECCLESIASTICAL JURISDICTION of the *diocese* of Rochester, and being a *peculiar* of the archbishop, is as such within the *deanry* of Shoreham. The church, which is situated in the ville of this parish, is dedicated to St. Martin. It consists of three isles and two chancels.

Among other monuments and inscriptions in it, are the following: *In the north and middle isles,* memorials for the Kidders. *In the great chancel,* memorials for the Bulls and Newmans; on the north side of the altar, a monument for Margaret, wife of Tho. Seyliard, daughter and heir of Francis Rogers, esq. of Otford,

q Guill. 204. Harl. MSS. No. 810-110. r Harris's Hist. Kent, p. 112.

who

who left fix children, obt. 1615; above, the arms of Seyliard, Azure, a chief ermine in a lozenge, with a number of quarterings; beneath the above is a beautiful altar tomb for Dorothy, daughter of William Crowmer, efq. of Tunftall, firft married to William Seyliard, of Brafted, by whom fhe left four fons and two daughters; 2dly, to Michael Beresford, efq. of Wefterham, by whom fhe left one fon and two daughters, ob. 1613. In the eaft window is a fhield, with the arms of Chrift church, Canterbury, impaling Parker. *In the north chancel*, a memorial for Margaret, daughter of the Hon. John and Abigail Verney, ob. 1733, æt. 17; and for George, eldeft fon of the Hon. George and Margaret Verney, 1698, æt. 7. A mural monument for Margaret Mennes, daughter and heir of Sir Matthew Mennes, K. B. and the lady Margaret Stuart, married, fecondly, to Sir John Heath; fhe left Margaret, her only daughter, ob. 1676. On the north fide, a ftately monument, on which is the figure of a judge, in his robes and cap, and on his right fide his lady, refting on cufhions, erected for Sir Robert Heath, juftice of the common pleas, obt. 1649; Margaret his wife, ob. 1647; beneath an infcription, fhewing that he was the fon and heir of Robert Heath, efq. by Anne, daughter and coheir of Nicholas Pofier, gent. by whom he left fix fons and one daughter; arms at top, Heath argent billettée gules, a crofs ingrailed of the fecond, with quarterings, which fhield is likewife in coloured glafs in a window over the monument. In the middle of the great chancel is a very antient grave ftone, on which was an infcription in brafs capitals of the 13th century, round the verge, now picked out, and illegible.

The church, is a rectory of the antient patronage of the fee of Canterbury, the archbifhop being the prefent patron of it. By an antient valuation, taken in the 15th year of king Edward I. this church was valued at forty marcs.[s]

By virtue of the *commiffion of enquiry* into the value of church livings, taken by order of the ftate, in 1650, it was returned, that Brafted was a parfonage, containing a houfe, fifty acres of glebe land, and feventy-eight acres of woodland, worth together thirty pounds per annum, and the tithes of the faid parfonage ninety pounds per annum; that it formerly was in the gift of the archbifhop of Canterbury, and that Mr. John Watte was then incumbent, put in by the parliament.[t]

[s] Stev. Mon. vol. i. p. 456.   [t] Par. Surv. Lam. lib. vol. xix.

This

This church is valued, in the king's books, at 22l. 6s. 8d. and the yearly tenths at 2l. 4s. 8d.

There was an inquisition taken concerning the glebe of this rectory, which had been withheld by the parishioners, and a decree on it was given by archbishop Islip, in 1352.[u]

CHURCH OF BRASTED.

PATRONS, Or by whom presented.	RECTORS.
Archbishop of Canterbury.............	Edmund de Mepham, S. T. P.[w]
	Andrew Pearson, B. D. about 1560.
	Thomas Bailey, about 1634.[y]
	John Saltmarsh, resig. 1646.[z]
	John Watte, in 1650.[a]
	.... Pinder, S. T. P.
	Robert Barker, S. T. P.
	Michael Bull, A.M. in 1723, ob. Aug. 27, 1763.[b]
	George Secker, S. T. P. 1763, ob. 1768.[c]
	James Parker, A. M. 1768, ob. July 1772.
	William Vise, S. T. P. inducted Jan. 5, 1773, resigned 1777.[1]
	Thomas Franklin, S. T. P. 1777, ob. Mar. 22, 1784.[e]
	Wm. Skinner, obt. Mar. 1795.
	George Moore, A.M. collated June, 1795. Present rector.[f]

[u] Reg. Islip. Lambeth library.

[w] He lies buried in the chancel of this church.

[x] He was also vicar of Wrotham and rector of Chidingstone.

[y] A man of great parts and profound learning, especially in the Greek tongue. He was sequestred from this rectory, worth 200l. per annum, in the time of the troubles; after the Restoration he was made dean of Downe, and afterwards, in 1664, bishop of Killala, as a reward for his sufferings and loyalty. Walk. Suff. of the Clergy, p. 202.

[z] He was a bigotted enthusiast. See much of him in Wood's Ath. vol. ii.

p. 287. He was put into possession of this rectory by the parliament.

[a] Put in likewise by the parliament.

[b] He lies buried in this church.

[c] He was nephew to abp. Secker, and was likewise canon residentiary of St. Paul's, and rector of Allhallows, Thames street. He had been before prebendary of Canterbury.

[d] He is a prebendary of Litchfield, and resigned this rectory on being presented to that of Lambeth, in Surry.

[e] Formerly Greek professor in the university of Cambridge, and vicar of Ware, in Hertfordshire.

[f] Prebendary of Canterbury, and son of archbishop Moore.

LOCAL HISTORY REPRINTS

Local History Reprints is a non-profit making publisher that reprints antiquarian, Victorian, Edwardian and other local history publications that are now out of print and unavailable.

It specialises in material of interest to the local and family historian, or those who wish to discover more about an area in which they are interested.

Books are published with the aim of promoting a greater awareness of a locality's heritage and encouraging research into its past.

A range of contemporary local histories are also published.

For details concerning the range of publications available please forward a stamped addressed envelope to the undermentioned address.

ISBN 1 85699 141 5

LOCAL HISTORY

316 GREEN LANE, STREATHAM, LOI

ISBN 1856991415

9 781856 991414